For Free and For Fun

How to Ask for the
Appointment and Get It

By Christopher Morrissette

About Christopher Morrissette

Chris started out his professional career as a shipbuilder building aircraft carriers for the US Navy. It was here that he learned the difference between a manufacturing culture and sales culture. After five years of shipbuilding he knew that there had to be a change. Chris asked "What am I *not* good at? I know I am not good at sales." And so his professional selling career began. Chris interviewed several sales companies and felt there was one sales manager that he could learn from more than the others. So he began to work with a "Fortune 500" sales company in 2000.

Chris' career was not all glory, he did have his highs and lows but eventually he became one of the top salespeople, regionally and nationally. After honing his skills it was time to move on professionally and start his own company, Easy Giving. This is where Chris continues to increase his skills and compete in the marketplace.

Chris started "For Free and For Fun," an educational company, after a friend of his asked how he was so effective in getting appointments. After a few minutes of instruction and role playing, Chris' friend called back the next day with extreme excitement where he had made five cold calls and booked three appointments. The bottom line is that his friend, a Chemistry PhD and a foreigner, was able to get the same results Chris got with the techniques of *For Free and For Fun*.

Chris' main passion is to help 1000 people earn $100,000/year or more in income. This is a lifelong goal and the sole purpose of www.forfreeandforfun.com.

Chris resides in Holly Springs, NC with his wife, Anna, of 10 years and four beautiful girls Alexis, Madison, Candice, and Jenna.

For Free and For Fun

How to Ask for the
Appointment and Get It

By Christopher Morrissette

The author may be contacted at the following address.

For Free and For Fun
PO Box 935
Holly Springs, NC 27540
866-280-4973
Chris@ForFreeAndForFun.com

CREDITS
Editorial assistance by Mike Rumble of Right Brained Creative Writing & Editing Services
Cover provided by Marketing Ministries

First Printing: December 2008
Printed in the United States of America

10 9 8 7 6 5 4 3 2 1

Dedicated to Kevin, whose influence has changed my life forever.

Thank You.

Table of Contents

Foreword
by Kelly Castor

Gimmicks! Magic Pills! Silver Bullets!

It seems everywhere you turn we are being offered the "shortcuts" and "quick solutions" to things that actually require effort and discipline. What you'll find enclosed in "For Free and For Fun" are real-life, fundamental tasks that are necessary to succeed in sales... in fact, in life.

From planning, to tactics, to mindset – the entire methodology is contained in this book. You'll not only discover the common practices to succeed, but also the steps in defining your product or service's worth to your potential clients.

You'll also learn how to say it to your prospects in a way that compels them to give you an opportunity to present your product or service on your terms... as a salesperson, what more can you ask for?

Take to heart the advice contained in the following pages and reap the benefits of serving more customers. You'll learn there is no replacement for the fundamental steps necessary to succeed. However, there are definitive practices that can have your activities be more effective and they can be... *For Free and For Fun!*

Kelly Castor
Author of *"The No-Nonsense Guide to Management Effectiveness."*

www.practicallessons.com

Introduction

Many people don't succeed in sales or in business because of one thing and one thing only. They will not put themselves in a position to win. People don't succeed because they will not do enough work to get the number of appointments needed to learn what they are really doing. Whether they are a business owner, a salesman, or a farmer, there is a process where you must plant seed into the ground (the prospect), water it (cultivate the relationship), and seed will mysteriously grow into the harvest (the sale). So, the only way to win is to lay down as much seed as possible.

The more seed the greater the harvest. It doesn't matter how much technology you have, how big your tractors are, or how cool your CRM software is. The only way to win is to plant seed with the expectation of a mighty harvest. Usually when a farmer plants, he will plant 4 to 5 seeds even though he only needs one. The reason is there is no way to tell which seed will grow, but he knows out of many, at least one will. The only way you can position yourself to win is by planting many seeds. The only way to win is to call on many prospects. By calling on many prospects you know you will increase your chances of picking up customers and creating a huge harvest.

You can't shortcut the shortcut. The bottom line is there are no shortcuts. People try to figure out all sorts of fancy ways to not go out and plant seed. They try to do everything possible and go out of their way not to make a cold call, not to say hello to someone new and not to plant seed.

I am a part of BNI group (Business Networking International) and their tag line is "The Cure for the Common Cold Call." There are hundreds of networking groups out there touting that referrals are the best way to build your business, and referrals are. There are many great books on how to network. But networking doesn't replace working, prospecting, and planting seed. Cold calling is the short term solution and referrals are the long term solution. You have to do cold calling and gain referrals. Cold calling pays the bills and referrals buy the luxuries.

Referrals do work, but they can take a long time to cultivate a relationship strong enough to have trust enough to eventually purchase. Networking gives people a false sense of being productive. Networking is too shaky to depend on when your business is new because you have to know the right people at the right time to give you the right referral at the right moment. When the stars are aligned then you might, just might, get the business. If anything, referrals can be a measure of how you treat your colleagues and your customers.

Although I have received some of my best customers through referrals, 97% of my customers came through cold calling and planting seed. And there is no better way to start a relationship than by introducing yourself personally to your prospect. You do have to have a mixture of both prospecting and referrals to be successful. Remember: cold calling pays the bills; referrals buy the luxuries.

There is no other way around it. You just have to plant a lot seed to reap a big harvest. You have to do a lot of work and call on a lot of prospects to be successful. I wrote this book to help people be more comfortable with themselves and cold calling. To turn cold calls into appointments, then to turn those appointments into referrals for more appointments. More appointments equal more presentations; more presentations equal more sales, plain and simple. So, I developed an easy and simple system to increase the number of appointments a person can set. This system will HELP you plant as many seeds as possible. For free resources go to www.ForFreeAndForFun.com

- 1 -

For Free and For Fun

One of my sales coaches early in my career relayed a short story to me I about a guy named Tom. Tom was a sales guy in the Midwest. And out of 33 sales reps, you guessed it, he was ranked 33. Tom was miserable; wasn't making any money; and was always worried about how he was going to pay his bills. He was so miserable; he dreaded going to work on Mondays. His failure wasn't attributed to the amount of work he did. He started early every morning; worked all day; and came home late in the evening. His relationships began to suffer because of the long hours he was putting in. His employer kept him because he did work, he did close business and his compensation was low overhead to the company. Tom's misery went on for about 3 years and he wasn't making any headway. Finally, he had decided he'd had enough!

Tom was done with the stress, the worry, the long hours, and the pain of not knowing where the next sale was going to come from. He was done with not knowing week to week how he was going to pay his bills. He was done with having nothing to show for the long hours. He was done with the drudgery. He decided he was going to put his 2-week notice in on the following Monday.

The day before, Tom went golfing with Jesse. As the two were making their way toward a dog-leg par 5, Jesse just happened to ask Tom how work was going. Tom then expressed all of his absolute misery and discontent and mentioned he was quitting the next morning.

Jesse, who had had no sales training or experience, asked Tom a few questions, the first being: "Do you know enough about the industry?" Tom's answer was, "Absolutely! I know more about our industry than anyone in the company!" Jesse's next question was, "Do you know enough about what you are offering?" Tom's answer was again a resounding "YES!" Jesse continued, asking, "So can you really HELP your customers?" Tom then went into a long dissertation about all of the reasons why he was better than the competition. Jesse then leaned back, glanced into the air, and then stared at Tom.

What Jesse said next changed Tom's life. Jesse said, "Well it sounds like you are spending all of your time thinking about how you can HELP yourself, and almost no time sharing with your prospect how you can HELP them.

Here is what I want you to do. Wait one week before you turn in your resignation. I want you to go out tomorrow morning and work for free. Yes, for free! You are not making anything anyways, so free is par for you. Go to work for free, and go out and see how many people you can truly HELP with your service. If you can't HELP them, tell them. But talk to them with the sole purpose of figuring out how to HELP without any benefit to yourself at all. And have fun while you're at it! You are wrapped up so tight, you would make me want to quit!" "GO TO WORK FOR FREE AND HAVE FUN! *If you are truly trying to HELP you can never do or say the wrong thing.* So relax. Talk to me next week about how it went."

The next week Tom sold more business than he had sold the previous 3 months. He went from the bottom of 33 sales people to number 1 in 6 months. It got to the point where Tom no longer did any cold calls. 100% of his business came from referrals where people were calling him to HELP them out.

Tom's largest sale was soon to come. Tom was prospecting a large restaurant chain whose president he happened to meet at one of the stores. While waiting at a booth with a soda, the president came over and sat down. Tom turned over his napkin and went into how he could

For Free and For Fun

HELP the restaurant be more efficient and profitable. After the 15 minute meeting the president got up and called the VP over and said, "I want you to sign all of the contracts and work out all the logistics to go exclusively with Tom." The restaurant chain had 450 individual locations across the United States and was worth several tens of thousands of dollars in commission.

Tom is now the leading sales manager for a Fortune 500 company. He has nearly quadrupled his original income and gets to travel and have fun HELPing his sales people be successful with the very same philosophy.

When you realize why you are standing in front of your prospect; when you realize you are here to HELP people in every way you can; your life changes... because the perspective of your relationships change. When you add value in someone else's life, this creates value in your life. When you give value to other people, those same people become more valuable to you.

Be intentional. As you leave your house today or tomorrow morning; leave with one purpose. Leave with the purpose you are going to HELP two people. Come to the conclusion it does not matter which two people you

HELP; you are just going to HELP two people. At the end of the week, I promise you, your whole life will be different.

For Free and For Fun

- 2 -

Go Help or Go Home!!!

You can never say or do the wrong thing if you are truly trying to help.

Once I realized this philosophy it took so much pressure off. I did not have to be masterfully skilled at saying the most perfect things. I did not have to learn all of the best closes or regurgitate all of my objection rebuttals down to the robotic level. I did not have to figure out ways to logically twist my customer into signing a contract. I only had to go out every day with the sole purpose of HELPing my prospects and customers. As Zig Ziglar has always said, "If you help enough people get what they want, then you will get what you want."

The only way to really compete in the market place is by HELPing. The world is so small with digitization and the internet, in a few seconds I can look up almost any company, any person, or any product on the planet. Your reputation does precede you. What separates you from the other 7 billion people in the world? What separates you from everyone else is the value you bring to your relationships. The more you *HELP* your customers, the more you HELP prospects, the more you create value in their life. Like a super energized electromagnet, customers will be pulled to you and beat down your door begging to buy from you. If you devalue your customers; they will look for any reason to drop you and switch to a competitor.

How can you HELP? I am sure there are several ways you can HELP your customers out right now. By offering better service, quality, lead times, availability (having it in stock,) convenience, less expensive per unit, overall less cost, reduce business impact, environmentally friendly, etc. These ideas are just a value proposition from you to your customer.

Write down what your value proposition is.

_____

_____

Write down how you can truly HELP your customer.

_____

_____

What is something your customers can only get from you and your company and nowhere else?

_____

_____

_____

Many times the answer to this question is only "YOU!" There has to be something only "YOU" can do for your customers they cannot get anywhere else. You should figure out what your value proposition is. Figure out how you HELP your customers. Then talk with your customers in terms of HELPing them in the ways you are capable.

It goes without saying, do not play games. HELPing your prospect is not cute or designed to be something you say as a matter a fact. A real value proposition is something YOU TRULY BELIEVE. If you do not believe what you are saying; or believe in your company; or your product, or your ability to HELP, then YOU NEED TO GO WORK SOMEWHERE ELSE. You are not only doing the company you work for and your prospect a disservice, but you are most importantly hurting yourself. If you do not BELIEVE and have total confidence you can HELP the prospect, the prospect WILL know it. The prospect WILL pick up on your self-doubt and NOT BELIEVE YOU.

There is a reason you don't believe in your company, product or service. The reason you don't believe is because there **IS** something wrong with your company. There **IS** something wrong with your product, or there **IS** something wrong with you. Why else would you feel this way? If there **IS** something wrong, what makes you believe it will get better? So, listen to why you don't believe. It may not necessarily be the wrong industry for you but maybe the wrong company.

Why don't you believe in your company? How is this going to get better? What needs to happen for your belief in your company to increase? Is this possible?

_____

_____

_____

_____

_____

_____

_____

_____

Why don't you believe in your product? How is this going to get better? What needs to happen for your belief in your product to increase? Is this possible?

_____

_____

_____

_____

_____

_____

_____

Why don't you believe in your ability to HELP? What needs to happen for your belief in yourself to increase?

_____

_____

_____

_____

_____

_____

_____

_____

For Free and For Fun

- 3 -

Selling is Stealing

To be very straight forward, it is OK to laugh and have fun. However, your primary focus should be to HELP your prospect by using you, your product and your services. Everything you communicate with your prospect should be with the idea you, your product or service can HELP them. If it doesn't HELP them then you are not allowed to SELL it to them. The biggest difference between SELLING and HELPING is when you SELL you hurt, when you HELP, you increase value.

You have heard the saying "He can sell ice to Eskimos." Is this what you really want to do? Take someone's money and give them something they don't need in return? You would be taking money out of the Eskimo's pocket to feed his family. You are making him poorer and literally taking food out of his infant's mouth. Are you proud of yourself? Does this make you happy? Are you satisfied? When you sold the Eskimo ice, he will eventually figure out he did not need the ice. He would be sure to tell everyone he knows how you took advantage of him. And eventually it would give a bad name to every ice seller in the industry. Can you think of industries that have this type of image? Used car sales? Credit card processing? So, why did you sell him the ice? Was it your intent to steal from him? Are you a thief?

If you are HELPing the Eskimo; you would share how you have HELPed other Eskimos in the past. How you HELPed them build their houses faster so they can get warmer sooner and their families will be safe from the threat of weather and wild animals. This is where you are making everyone's life better. You HELPed the Eskimo have safety, shelter and warmth. You HELPed the Eskimo economy because you had to stay the night in an Eskimotel (yeah I know it's funny, just made it up – true story.) You HELPed your company stay in business longer as a supplier and you were HELPed because you made money to feed your family. Not to mention the Eskimo will be so excited he did not have to cut the blocks of ice himself, he will be more than happy to REFER everybody he knows so you can HELP them out as well. By HELPing the Eskimo, you will be literally creating a whole ice carving industry. If you just SELL you can destroy a family; you can destroy an entire industry. Look to create value for your customers. Look to truly HELP them.

- 4 -

Do Not Believe Your Own BS

"Do Not Believe Your Own BS #1"

Do not believe your own "B.S." Let me be very plain and simple here. <u>DO NOT LIE!</u> Do not tell half truths. Do not warp or twist the truth. Do not even play semantics... it doesn't matter if "it depends on what your definition of 'is' is." Whenever you twist, warp or use clever wording, your customer will eventually figure out your "cleverness" especially when they go to pay the invoice. Your "cleverness" will result in the customer not trusting you. If they do not trust you, they will not believe you are capable of fulfilling your end of the deal. Your customer will cancel the contract or not give you the second order.

If you are #1 in an area be proud of it, you earned it. If you are #2, be proud of being #2. Treat your weakness as strength but never lie about how you can HELP. The point is not to lie, because you are misleading the customer; the point is not to lie or stretch the truth because – lying will hurt YOU. Lying will attack your self-image. Lying will destroy how you FEEL about yourself. Lying will hurt your relationships and your business. You will continue to feel worse until you can't feel at all. Then you will be no good to anyone... you will be nothing more than a thief; SELLing and stealing.

When you lie, stretch the truth, or intentionally mislead; something happens inside of you which dissolves a little chink of your armor. Lie enough and your whole armor will be totally destroyed. You will no longer be able to do battle in the marketplace. When you lose your armor, the next blow you take will be your last. You no longer are capable of withstanding the onslaught of competitive forces attacking you. There is nothing left to buffer you from the sword of your competitor. You will die.

A customer leaves you because of: a broken promise, a back order, a missed deadline, a shipping issue, defects, wrong order, etc. Ladies and gentlemen, these "last straw" issues do not have to be your own fault. This last straw can happen outside your realm of control. Then you go blaming everyone and everything else as to why you lost this customer. Pretending this <u>ONE</u> "shipping issue" is why your customer refuses to do business with you. Forgive me; I don't know how else to say it, "Don't believe your own B.S." You did not lose this customer because of a "shipping issue." You lost this customer because <u>they</u> no longer believed <u>you</u> could HELP them. They no longer trusted <u>you</u> because of <u>YOUR</u> past inconsistencies; not the "last straw" issue which finally confirmed their decision to run into the arms of your competitor.

If it is not true then don't say it. Keep it to yourself. Do not trump things up. Be creative in what your #1 in, but do not lie to your customer or yourself.

"Do Not Believe Your Own BS #2"

Do not believe your own B.S. degree. Do not believe in your own <u>B</u>ook <u>S</u>marts. I have met many well educated people which have so much confidence in their education to the point they almost feel superior to others. There is almost an arrogance about them. A superior attitude is fine if you are applying for a job or a professorship or you are running for political office. But arrogance has no place in front of a prospect. To a prospect your education means absolutely nothing. The prospect does not care at all how educated you are. You could have your master's degree or your PhD. You could have more degrees than a thermometer. Your name could be Mr. or Mrs. Fahrenheit! The prospect does not care about who you are or what you have done... they only care how you can HELP them now. If you can't HELP them; then go home. Your prospect will gladly show you the door.

"Do Not Believe Your Own BS #3"

Do not believe your own <u>B</u>ody <u>S</u>tructure. "Pretty Boys" don't make it. People who believe they will get by on their good looks will be very disappointed in the end. Yes, you may have enough looks, charm and charisma to get an initial appointment, but you better come strong with value or you will lose every time. I have noticed through the years that pretty boys and girls rely so much on their looks they feel no need to work. Only "work" will make you successful. Even models put in 12 to 15 hours days with travel, working out and photo shoots. Pretty people rarely succeed without doing *everything* it takes to be successful.

Do not believe your own <u>B</u>ody <u>S</u>tructure. If you are overweight; accept you are overweight. If you are "fat" then face the fact you are "fat". Get bigger clothes that fit right. Lose weight if you are uncomfortable with yourself. Your being overweight has nothing to do with how successful you. You can HELP people no matter what you look like. I have met multi-millionaires who are clearly overweight but they are still successful. So get over yourself, they have.

"Do Not Believe Your Own BS #4"

Do not believe your own negative Belief System. Baggage Sucks! Leave your baggage at home; get over yourself. Get out of your own way. You should believe you can HELP out every prospect you talk to. If you didn't think you would be able to HELP the prospect as a customer then why would you waste your time calling them? It is easy to believe if you do one call then you would make one sale, and doing 2 sales calls would result in 2 sales. What about going 3 for 3? 5 for 5? 10 for 10? 20 sales calls and making 20 sales? At what point do you start believing it is not feasible to make the sale? At what point do you start doubting your ability?

Check yourself. The moment you stop believing is the point where your own baggage begins. This is where your negative belief system starts and lets you know what you think about yourself and your success. Your past does not equal your future. Let's move on.

Think like an Insurance Company

"Sales" is a numbers game and you should know your percentages of sales calls to closes. What I have noticed with sales people is they do a sales call and they don't make a sale. They do another sales call and they don't make another sale. They do another sales call and they don't make another sale. They continue this cycle and finally begin to believe the next person they call on, they will not be able to HELP either. They eventually believe no one needs their HELP. Then they quit; emotionally first, then physically. If you think too much about the results, then you will not be productive.

The results are not as important as the work. If you do the work the results will come. The fact is if you thought like an insurance company, the more calls you did the more excited you would become. The way insurance companies determine levels of risk and the amount of premiums to charge is this. They take all the factors and put them into a formula which says out of "X amount of tries" statistically a particular event will have to happen at least once. They know at least 1 out of 5000 people will lose their house to fire and they plan for it. They know *someone* out of a 5000 will lose their home. They just don't know *who*. And you do not either.

If you think like an insurance company you will begin to see for every person who does not want your service the closer you are coming to actually finding the person who will need you. The question is not *if* someone's house will go up in smoke, it is a question of *when*. And the insurance companies know their numbers to the point where it is not even a question of *when*, but *who*. Insurance companies have full confidence someone is going to have to use their service. You need to have the same absolute confidence. For every person who does not use your product or service you are so much closer to finding one who will. It is not a question of *if* someone will use your service but a question of *when and who*.

The Power of Integrity

When you are blameless with absolute integrity and you have done everything you said you would do; you can say to the new prospect "all I have said I would do; I have done." They will feel the strength, the confidence and the power in your words. If you have climbed Mount Everest and you tell them you have, you can speak from full experiential memories. It actually happened and when you talk about it, you will maintain the captivated interest of your audience. This absolute faith and strength is what your customers pick up on. They use YOUR conviction to HELP make decisions about you, your company and your products.

If you say you climbed Mount Everest and you only climbed the hill in your back yard then your power is diminished. Your voice, body language, saliva in your throat, your tongue thickening, your pupils dilating, and your forehead glistening with perspiration are all signs you are not comfortable with your words. Your prospect will know you are not telling the truth. They may not be able to pick up on it exactly but they will have a "gut feeling" there is something missing from the story. They will know something is missing from the experience you are discussing. Do not allow your prospect or customer to have a "gut feeling" something is not right. They will eventually have the "gut feeling" not to pay you.

When I talk to prospects I know from absolute experience I have saved companies thousands of dollars, while developing a plan to motivate their sales teams and increase employee loyalty. I know this is true and the prospect FEELS it is true also. They place the order to at least try to experience the feeling I have shared with them.

If you are speaking the truth say it with full confidence, conviction and strength. When you are speaking the truth... then by all means YELL it from the roof tops. Ring a bell, Sound the alarms... you are not **"showing off"** by being truthful you are **"sharing off."** You are creating a sense of security for your customer which they know beyond a shadow of a doubt you are capable of HELPing them. Your new customer is buying this sense of security not necessarily the product you offer.

For Free and For Fun

- 5 -

Open Up and Say "Ahhh!!"

Relax

The more relaxed you are, the more confidence and conviction you exude. If you are anxious everyone will pick up on it and they will be hesitant to do anything you ask. For some reason it is human nature to not want to do what others want you to do. This is true especially when people are very interested and anxious for you to do something. Gentlemen, you know what I mean. When your wife asks you to do something, is your first inclination to do it? No, probably not. If it was your idea then you would have been excited to paint the dining room an ugly greenish-cream color. But because painting was someone else's idea your excitement to do the task is severely diminished. This is true in anything, especially sales.

Before I make a call on a prospective client, I remind myself of the following:

1. Take a deep breath and blow out the anxiety.

For Free and For Fun

2. I am human and I am talking to another human – this reminds me we are all the same.   We all have the same wants, desires, and fears. CEO's and Exec VP's have the same fears and desires as anyone else. I remind myself we all get dressed the same way in the morning. ***There are no great people; there are just ordinary people that have made great decisions.***

3. Have a conversation. We will go into a sales script later, but I need to know it enough to own it. It will guide the conversation, but not seem canned. I pretend I am professionally talking with my best friend.

4. It is only a cold call the first time I walk in. From there on out, they know me. If they like me or not this is a different subject entirely, but they do know me.

5. If I can HELP, then they need me to call; how else are they going to know how I can HELP? I know I can really HELP them or why else would I call?

Have Fun

The world has enough stuffy, boring, and obnoxious people. When you have fun you are exciting to be around and people really enjoy your company. The more fun you have the more people will be attracted to you and the more you will be able to accomplish.

One day when I was cold calling I walked into an office building. I was met with a very unique experience. Susan was behind the desk. Susan said very sternly "We don't allow soliciting!" I said "That's OK ma'am, I quit a couple of years ago, very bad habit, and it was making me real sick! I am Chris with Easy Giving and I HELP companies... who do you recommend I speak with?" After a minute or two Susan had understood what I had said (I pretended to think that she said "We don't allow 'smoking'). She immediately burst out laughing so hard she came to tears. She looked at me and gave me Bill's card, the decision maker. Susan said with a huge grin and a wink "Here is his card; you earned it, now get out of here." It is OK to be a little corny.

Have fun; it is OK not to be normal. It is OK to be goofy and not have all of the answers. It is OK to say something stupid on accident or on purpose in my case. It is OK to laugh at yourself and the circumstances you are in. ***Remember you can never do or say the wrong thing if you are truly trying to HELP.***

The whole philosophy of 'For Free and For Fun' is to create a mindset you can and should HELP. As you get better and learn more you will find more ways to HELP. This is an obligation on your part to your prospects and customers. The reason you are calling on them in the first place is you know you *can* HELP.

Incidentally, when you HELP more people you will make more money because you have become more valuable. With this mindset you are able to call on anyone, from the CEO down to the middle manager, to make an appointment because you know you will be able to somehow make their life better.

- 6 -

Why Do I Care?

This is what your prospect is thinking the entire time you are talking to them. You sound just like Charlie Brown's teacher when you talk about how long your company has been in business, how fancy your product is or tell them how long you have been in the industry. Your customer does not care. Why should they? If you do not share how you can HELP them you are wasting their time. Your customer only cares how you can HELP them.

What Do You Really Offer? How Do You HELP?

I have asked many sales people what they sell. Their responses vary based on the industry but it always seems to be product or service oriented. They sell cell phones, CRM software, switches and routers, multifunction machines, lawn care services, organizing services, and accounting, etc.

For Free and For Fun

We, as sales people, do not sell products or services. Our customers could care less about what we sell. Our customers are only concerned about what they get out of purchasing our product or service.

If you sell:

- Accounting – you HELP save people time and money with their taxes.

- Lawn Care Services – you HELP save people time and add value to their homes.

- Multi-function machines – you HELP with convenience and productivity.

- Cell phones – you HELP with convenience and accessibility to family, friends, and customers.

- Hotel rooms – you HELP with convenience and productivity.

How you HELP is not what you put into your product or service, but what your customer gets out of it.

So how can you help? Take a minute right now and list 5 ways, other than money, you and your company can HELP and increase your customers' quality of life?

1. _____

2. _____

3. _____

4. _____

5. _____

For Free and For Fun

How many different industries can you HELP with your product/service? List the industries and how you can HELP them?

1. _____

2. _____

3. _____

4. _____

5. _____

Now list 5 ways you have specifically HELPed a real customer in the past.

1. _____

2. _____

3. _____

4. _____

5. _____

What different services or products can you HELP your customers with?   Now what do they get out of your product?

1. _____

2. _____

3. _____

4. _____

5. _____

For Free and For Fun

- 7 -

Asking for the Appointment and Getting It

Why is it Called 'Cold Calling' if it Makes us Sweat? Shouldn't it be Called 'Hot Calling?'

People usually get emotionally hung up on the idea of walking into someplace they have never been and talking to someone they have never met. The simple truth is; *it is only a cold call the first time you introduce yourself.* After the first time the prospect knows you. If they like you or not is a different thing entirely, but they still know who you are. Think of your best friend... did you know your best friend before you knew him? No, of course not. So, when you introduced yourself the first time there was probably a small moment of awkwardness. The second time you spoke the awkwardness was gone because you picked up from where you left off.

This is also true with our spouses. When I first met my wife there was some awkwardness. When I called her later to talk, we were able to pick back up where we left off. When we spoke the third time there was a continued familiarity.

This familiarity is also true with prospects. This familiarity is continued the second call, meeting or visit. The third call you get to start where you left off from the first two calls. So, don't get hung up on the cold call. The trade off is two minutes of awkwardness for a lifetime of friendship and business.

Cold Call to Appointment in 5 Minutes or Less

5 Seconds of Fame, Baby!

Why should your prospect listen to you? You only get 5 seconds for prospects to make a value judgment on whether they should listen to you another 5 seconds. In those 5 seconds you need to tell them:

1. Who you are?

2. Who you are with?

3. Who you have HELPed.

4. How you can HELP them specifically.

5. Ask for the appointment to share how you can HELP.

The Purpose of Cold Calling – Just Walking in the Door

The only purpose of the cold call is to find out whom to make an appointment with.

Go in with absolutely no sales materials, no pricing, no literature, no computer and no bags! The only things to bring in are business cards, a pen, a calendar and a smile! Business cards are to trade with the person you speak with. A pen is to write down the name of the person you speak to on the back of the decision maker's business card. Your calendar is there in case you run into the person you need to make an appointment with. This allows you to immediately make an appointment without having to call back (this is very efficient.) And a smile... the fastest, easiest and most inexpensive way to look 10 times more attractive is to have a genuine smile when you say "Hello."

Approaching the Gate Keeper:

"Hello I am Chris with Easy Giving. I help companies get a greater return with their employee appreciation gifts and incentives. Even though you can't tell, I do run off appointments. I wanted to know who you would recommend I make an appointment with? They say "Do you have a card?" Then I say "Can I trade you?" "Can you let Bob know I will give him a call tomorrow afternoon? I am sorry, what was your name ma'am?" "Thank you so much Cindy, I appreciate your HELP and have a great week."

This is your five seconds of fame. About 80% to 90% of the time the front desk person will give you the person's name you need to speak with, if for no other reason than to get you out of the office.

If you do speak with the decision maker, go into the next conversation. Even if you meet the decision maker in the hallway, you still are just asking for an appointment. Just because you accidentally met him on the way to the restroom does not mean he was expecting you and has put time aside for a meeting! (hahaha!) If he has time and the issue is eminently important to him, he will ask you to talk about how you can HELP him.

Caution! You know how long your presentation is. Ask the prospect if he has the amount of time necessary to do your complete presentation. If the prospect says "Yes," then by all means share how you can HELP right then. If he does not have the amount of time needed available, you should make an appointment to come back. If it really does take 40 minutes to go through how you can HELP, what makes you think the prospect will be able to make a clear decision on 20 minutes of information?

When You Call Back

The only purpose of the phone call is to make an appointment.

"Hey Bob, I am Chris with Easy Giving. Do you have a quick second? Did I call you at a good time?" Bob says, "This is OK, go ahead." "Thank you I always like to ask. Cindy recommended I give you a quick call. I HELP nursing homes get a greater return on their employee appreciation gifts and incentives. What I would like to do is make a brief appointment with you to share how I HELP my customers out and to see if I would be a benefit to you as well." <Let a pause go on> "What does your schedule look like?" <Just shut up here and let the prospect tell you when he is available. Make the appointment. If you talk here you will screw it up.> "Thank you Bob, I will be there!

I am looking forward to meeting with you to see how I can HELP, have a great week."

If you go into voicemail leave a message! With all the technology out there, if you hang up, they still know you called. The next time your prospect is at their desk they will recognize your number and they will remember you hung up on their voicemail five times already. So they will definitely not take your call this particular time.

I have had many prospects I finally got to talk with say "Yes, Chris, I have received your voicemails." This has allowed me to ask for an appointment because of their familiarity with me. I will go into the thought process and particulars of leaving voicemails; the how's and when's later.

For Free and For Fun

- 8 -

The 5 Second Introduction Dissected

1. **"I am Chris."** Who are you? Only use your first name in the introduction. The first reason is your last name takes another second of time to say and is wasteful because most people don't care who you are. The second reason is it helps establish a little bit of rapport. If you only use your first name then it moves you a little closer to a friendship.

   Using your first name takes down a little part of the wall. Remember people buy from people they like. When is the last time you called your best friend and said "this is Chris Morrissette, is Derek Jenson there?" No, you barely introduce yourself and just use their first name if you use their real name at all. When you are great friends, you probably don't even introduce yourself when you call and you barely even ask for him. You say "Hey, is Billy Bob there?" or "Whatssup, can John talk?" If you feel the need to call them Sir or Mr. Jackson by all means please do so. But only introduce yourself by your first name. Be on a first name basis with your prospect and they will like you sooner.

2. **"with Easy Giving."** Who you are with? If you are #1 on Wall Street, #1 in your industry or #1 in your backyard you need to say your company name as if it were a household name. You need to be proud of it. As if to say to your prospect "you haven't heard of us? I am sooooo surprised! Wow that is a first!" But don't say this of course; just be proud of your company. "I am Chris with Easy Giving!"

3. **"Do you have a quick second? Did I call at a good time?"** Be considerate of what you may be interrupting. If the prospect says this is a bad time then politely ask when you can call back and say "I will do it and talk to you then!" Then do not say anything more about who you are and what you do... JUST GET OFF THE PHONE!

You will gain more respect and attention by allowing the person to get you off the phone quickly than you ever will by trying to rush through your five second introduction. If you do rush, your prospect is not paying attention to you. The prospect will only be focused on one thing – getting you off the phone so they can get back to what they were doing. If you do rush through your introduction, I guarantee you will not get the appointment.

I know your five second intro to ask for an appointment only takes five seconds but it is the air and attitude in which you are listened to which is most important. If a person is busy on the other end, then they will not be listening to you, no matter how fast you can ramble off who you are and why you are calling.

If you ask them if it is OK to talk and they say "YES," then you have the right to take deep breath and talk relaxed, person to person. This allows you to have a real conversation to introduce yourself, how you can HELP and ask for an appointment. If you rush your introduction you seem nervous or anxious.

If you are nervous, the perception is you are just unsuccessfully peddling stuff and why would they want to talk to you? Asking if they have a quick second allows them to say "No" and you to relax. Being relaxed in sales breeds the confidence and conviction you need to let the prospect know you are worth their time to talk with.

4. **"Cindy recommended I give you a call."**

Now Cindy is the person you met at the front desk, remember? This is why you wrote her name down on the back of Bill's card she gave you. So you could remember who recommended you call Bill. This statement acts as an implied referral. And remember use just her first name; chances are her first name is all you could pay attention to anyways. This statement lends a little more credibility to who you are. The prospect thinks to a certain extent, "Well if Cindy recommended you call; then you must have something of value. She is trained to keep people away from me." Very few times will someone ask "How do you know Cindy?" Then I say "I stopped in last week and mentioned to her how I have been able to HELP my customers and she recommended I give you a call." Remember you still want to be truthful. The kiss of death in any relationship is a lack of trust – and this goes for selling as well.

5. **"I HELP…'companies; policeman; chemical manufacturers; IT departments, doctor's offices, apartment complexes, etc.'"**

The point here is you have to figure out WHO your customers are you HELP out.   Try to cite the industry or group name you HELP specifically in relation to your prospect. This will let the prospect know it is probably a good idea to listen to you because you have HELPed the radio station in another city if the prospect is a radio station.

If you are a police officer and I sell life insurance then I would tell you "I HELP police officers." It does not matter to you I also HELP teachers, carpenters and corporate executives with their insurance. It only matters to you I have HELPed other police officers. This gives me credibility. Since I have HELPed other police officers then you would think I probably could HELP you.

If you are calling on a law firm, you would let them know you have HELPed other law firms. If you are calling on a tire manufacturing plant, you would relate to them you have HELPed other tire manufacturing plants. If you are calling on small businesses you would let them know you have HELPed other small businesses.

Be as specific as you possibly can. You can be creative here and still be truthful. If you haven't HELPed a police officer but a fireman instead then you could say you have HELPed "public servants." Just make sure you relate WHO you have helped to the prospect you are speaking with.

6. **"I HELP police officers with... 'saving time, making sure they have proper coverage, save money on their existing coverage, etc.'"**

This is your value proposition. Not only do you HELP other police officers but you have HELPed them specifically in an area of their concern. This means you must know a little bit about who you are talking to. You must at least know enough about your prospect to understand their hot buttons. Remember, "Go HELP or

Go Home." Maybe police officers experience a lot of denied policies or sky high premiums because of the safety risk of their work. You can HELP them reduce their premiums and HELP them get the proper coverage. With this scenario I would say, "I HELP police officers make sure they are properly covered and I have been able to HELP many reduce their premiums." None the less, if this doesn't fit your example, there has to be some way you HELP your customers. Think about it and use your example.

7. **Mental Note: You might want to have a list of your customers ready.** Every one out of ten calls; the prospect will ask, "Well, who are your customers?" It is usually sufficient to list three to four companies which are close to them either geographically or in the same industry. Again, use the company's exact info. "Well Bob, I HELP Harold Johnson over at XYZ Manufacturing in Durham. I take care of Jenny at Jenny Enterprises in Raleigh. I have been able to HELP Jim Simpson at the Cary Fire Department."

If you know your prospect, just name a few of your customers they would more than likely know. If you are working with BIG names then feel free to say you have BIG name clients. If the name of your customer is BIG and your prospect is small then you may want to give one BIG name for credibility and two small names which are closer to the business model and size of your prospect. None the less, a list of customers in front of you by company name, city and contact will save you on more than one occasion.

Side bar – don't lie or embellish here, no matter how tempting it may be. If you give the name of a company and a contact you don't know, the prospect just may know Bill at XYZ Manufacturing. It is a small world. If you are pushed into it, just tell the prospect very plainly if you can HELP them; they would be the very first person in the industry you have HELPed. This is reasonable. You couldn't possibly have a customer in every size, market, or industry. The prospect knows you don't also and they will appreciate your forthrightness and candidness. I would say "Well Bob, you would be the first company/customer I have in this area but I do take care of Karen at Johnnies Restaurant in Smithfield, does that count?" By asking "Does that count?" the prospect will almost always invariably say yes.

8. **"I would like to make a brief appointment with you and 'share' how I HELP my customers. To see if I can benefit you as well."** Ask for the appointment by offering to *share*; or "I would like to make a brief appointment and share with you how I have been able to HELP other police officers." Because you are offering to SHARE how you HELP your other customers in their industry, this is very disarming and people really do want HELP. If you are offering HELP then your prospects really do want YOUR HELP. People are looking for advice and solutions on how to do things better and more efficiently. When you make this statement you are just asking to sit down and share how you can HELP them.

9. **The Pause** – this is necessary because you just finished talking for 5-10 seconds and you need to let the other person digest all of what you have said. If you jump right into when to make an appointment it seems real "salesy." It appears you are too anxious. Remember if you are too anxious there will be a strong tendency for your prospect not to want to do anything

you ask them to. So take a deep breath here and PAUSE. This will also allow you to relax and give the prospect enough time to think. Don't rush the conversation, just let it be natural. You wouldn't rush a conversation with a friend would you?

10. **Ask for when and where to meet.** In a very relaxed and confident voice ask for an appointment. It is OK to joke around here, but make sure you are relaxed. Remember you are HELPing them. You are just trying to figure out the calendar details.

11. **"Thank you Bob"** – appreciate him and his time. This goes a long way in your prospect respecting you and your time. If you appreciate and respect him then chances are he will appreciate and respect you.

12. **"I will be there!"** – Say this as concrete and definite as you can without raising your voice. This creates a definite appointment time in the mind of the prospect because you just gave a very strong verbal commitment. This is confirmation #1 of the

appointment. You are making a commitment to him and people normally reciprocate.

13. **"I am looking forward to meeting you and seeing how I can HELP."** This creates anticipation and expectation on the part of the prospect. How many times has someone called you and said they are looking forward to seeing how they can HELP you? This reminds the prospect why he needs to meet with you. This is appointment confirmation #2.

14. **"I will see you at the Holiday Inn on Tuesday. Have a great week."** This is appointment confirmation number #3.

After doing all this... I really hope you have something of value to offer because your prospect is sure expecting you to have it! Good luck on the presentation.

For Free and For Fun

- 9 -

Build an Appointment Script for Yourself

Use the list of questions below to build your script. You will have a separate script for each type of customer you call on but all your scripts will have the same elements. This is a skeleton outline to use.

1. Who are you? "I am _____ ,"

2. Who are you with? "with _____ ."

3. Do you have a second? Did I call at a good time?

4. Who recommended you call? "_____ recommended I give you a call."

5. Who do you HELP? "I HELP _____ "

6. How do you HELP? "with

    _____

    _____

    _____

    _____."

7. "I would like to make a brief appointment with you and share how I HELP my customers. To see if I can be a benefit to you as well."

8. **Pause**

9. "When would you like me to come by for a few minutes?"

10. "Thank you _____."

11. "I am looking forward to seeing how I can HELP."

12. "I will see you later this week."

How To Ask For the Appointment and Get It

Take a moment and write your appointment script:

_____

_____

_____

_____

_____

_____

_____

_____

_____

For Free and For Fun

- 10 -

To Leave or Not to Leave
a Voicemail – That is the Question?

We have all been there. In spite of our best efforts, we have called and was captured by the gate keeper only to be shoved into the voicemail graveyard. I recommend always leaving messages. They will still know you called if you leave a message or not. If you leave a message it states you are PROUD of what you have to offer and you believe you can HELP them. If you don't leave a message they will feel the opposite.

Some Tips:

1. Be sincere – you are calling because you know you can HELP them.

2. Be enthusiastic and upbeat – they are just getting back from lunch because you left them a message at 12:15pm. So don't put them to sleep.

For Free and For Fun

3. Be very distinct and speak clearly with confidence. You may have to get off your Bluetooth earpiece for this one. I have found a number of messages to be garbled by Bluetooth to voicemail. I don't know why; just consider it a "mystery of life."

4. Say the prospect's name 4 times – people like their name and they will pay more attention to your voicemail because you are leaving the message specifically to THEM.

5. Give your phone number at the beginning of the message, and at the end of it too. The way voicemail messages work; the prospect did not pay attention to your phone number the first time. The prospect did not pay attention because they did not realize it was valuable to do so. So, leave your number at the end slowly. The reason you leave the number at the beginning of the message is when they "replay" your message to get your number, they won't have to listen to the entire message again to write your number down. Your number at the beginning and end of a message also covers saying your number twice in case one of the numbers did not sound clear.

6. When you say your phone number, again be very clear and distinct. We get so used to saying our contact information that we can literally rattle it off without taking a breath while cornering a turn, changing the radio station and drinking our coffee as we drive off into traffic. Our prospects don't know us well enough to be able to recognize our information when we rattle it off. People have left me messages where they said their number so fast, I could not understand what number to call back. So, I replayed the message 10 times and eventually got frustrated and deleted the message. And this was a person I WANTED to call back. Can you imagine what I would have done if I did not want to call the person back? You guessed it; I would have been going for the world record time of deleting a message and forwarding on to the next one.

7. Keep track of when you leave messages by taking notes. Anyone important enough for you to call is important enough for you to note WHEN you called them. This way you can track how frequently you call them to space them out properly.

8. When you track messages; you should also take notes on what you talked about. Nothing is more embarrassing than to congratulate someone on their child's graduation only to be reminded their oldest child is only 3 years old! Yeah, I would back track and recover pretty well by saying "I do remember you telling me how smart she was! I just thought, with her intelligence, she was almost done with school." It is still better if you don't have to back pedal. So take notes.

Voicemail Wording and Frequency

The wording is very similar to the actual appointment script but it is shorter and more upbeat. **"Hi Ben, Cindy recommended I give you a quick call. I am Chris with Easy Giving 866-280-4973 and I help companies…. Ben, I just wanted to make a brief appointment with you to see if I can help you as well. My number is 866-280-4973. If I don't talk with you today, then I will give you a quick shout tomorrow afternoon. Thank you Ben, I am looking forward to seeing how I can help."** <I mark this as voicemail #1 and note the date in my notes.>

By telling the prospect you will call back at a particular time, you are in an odd sort of way making an appointment with them. By you calling them back you are actually "keeping your promise." By doing this continually; you are building credibility. You promote the idea you will do what you say.

My next message is **"Hey Bill, just calling back as 'promised.' I HELP….. just wanted to make an appointment with you; sorry I missed you. I know I can HELP. I will give you a call three days from now (I would say next Tuesday or Wednesday whatever is three to four days away)."** <I mark this as voicemail #2 and note the date.>

This actually begins to set some reference in the prospect's mind that you are good for your word and gives the right to keep your "promise" again.

Message number 3 is **"Hey Bill, calling you back as promised. I know I can HELP with... I have HELPed a few of these companies like... and... and I wanted to see if I could HELP you as well. My number is 866-280-4973. I tell you what Bill, my goal is not to fill up your voicemail, even though it may seem like it. <It's OK to laugh here> I know you got a lot going on, so I will give you a call about** a week from now to see if we can touch base. If you need me sooner; you got me. 866-280-4973. Talk to you then."

This is a personal message from you to the prospect stating you can HELP and you have specifically HELPed others in the area. You have also set another "appointment" to call back.

Sooner or later, about 70% of the time, you will get to talk to the person you are leaving messages for. These people, if you are nice and polite on the phone, will eventually talk with you. In a weird sort of way, because you have left so many upbeat messages, they actually feel like they know you. When you eventually talk with them you have a 90% chance of getting an appointment. I have done this scenario many times. I have left up to 10 messages over a 4 month period with a pharmaceutical company and they eventually became a customer.

Mental Note: It doesn't matter how long you have been calling on them, when you do get them on the phone hold your excitement down and don't rush. Start into the appointment script. **"Do you have a second? Did I catch you at a good time?"** There is no worse feeling in the world to finally get the decision maker on the phone and to rush through everything and not get the appointment because you were too anxious.

Remember, not to be too anxious...

For Free and For Fun

- 11 -

Call Windows

There are two distinct call windows to actually get people at their desk. The first window is between 10am and 11:15am and the second window is from 2pm to 3:15pm. For whatever reason (just call it a "mystery of life"), people are usually at their desk in these time frames. Before 10am, people seem to be getting their share of coffee and office gossip and after 11:15am, people are getting ready to go to lunch. Same thing for before 2pm, people are coming back from lunch and after 3:15pm, people are getting ready to go home. I wonder how we can keep our economy afloat with only 2.5 hours of work done a day. It is really less than 2.5 hours... remember, because YOU are calling and interrupting them... AMAZING!

Depending on who you are prospecting you may have to change your strategy a little. Here are a few tips to reach different populations. Every industry has its own little nuances. You will have to figure out what works for your business.

1. C-Level and VP contacts:

If you really need to get a hold of these people I would recommend calling on the "6's" – around 6am and 6pm. Most CEO's and VP's are driven people. Being driven is how they got to where they are. So, if you called at these times you would have a greater chance of getting through to them because the gatekeeper doesn't normally get to the office until 7am at the earliest. The gatekeeper normally leaves around 5pm. So, the gatekeeper will be in the car and not defending the post.

A caveat to this is if you called at 6am, the CEO would realize you are as driven or as crazy as they are. Just on this idea alone you would have a higher likelihood to get an appointment. If anything, you would definitely get their respect. By the way you deserve their respect... how many days have you put in from 6am to 6pm? Because you are willing to do more than most; you are able to HELP more than your competition.

2. If you are selling to the general public:

If you called at 12pm or 5:15pm, people would be more apt to pick up their cell phone. Most people are in their car driving to lunch or on the way home which can be a boring event. So, they will pick up the phone call just out of curiosity, wondering who is calling. People are looking for distractions or entertainment to pass the time. When they do pick up; talk and ask for an appointment. You can still ask for an appointment while they are driving. You can suggest to them you will send an email to their office/home email to remind them to put the appointment in their calendar. Now when you hang up get on your phone and send an email! What? Don't have email on your phone? Sorry, good luck on remembering to remind the prospect of the appointment when you get home. Technology... it's a beautiful thing!

3. Know the habits of people in the industry you call on:

i. If you are selling to manufacturers then know their normal hours for first shift are 7am to 3:30pm. Their lunch usually lasts only about 30 minutes and the times can be staggered between 10:30am to 12:30pm.

ii. If you sell to restaurants, then you have quickly figured out between 11:30am and 2pm is the lunch rush, and you can really blow an opportunity with a restaurant by interrupting them at this time. To say the least, they would not be happy with you if you called or stopped by between those hours.

iii. If you are selling to a nursing home, then calling or going by at 10am is the best time, because they are usually done with their morning management meetings by then.

Presentation

There are thousands of books on the presentation part of the sales cycle with all of the objections and the "feel, felt, found" responses. Here are a few excellent books on teaching how to do a presentation and handle objections.

- *How to Master the Art of Selling* by Tom Hopkins

- Zig Ziglar's *Secrets of Closing the Sale*

- *The Sales Bible* by Jeffrey H. Gitomer

Ok, now you have a new customer after an appointment and the presentation. Congratulations! Don't go to Disneyland yet. You are not done. To maximize the sales call you should then ask for referrals if you HELP them out as a customer or not.

What? I can ask for a referral even though I did not HELP the prospect?

Yes you can!

For Free and For Fun

- 12 -

Referrals – Ask for Them!

Where cold calling is an immediate short term approach to increase your prospect pipeline, referrals are a rich long term resource to increase your business' stability. All referrals are based on trust. With some people, you have the ability to gain trust on the first meeting, and with others, it can take years of constantly proving yourself. Either way, if you are not asking for referrals, then you are wasting your time. If you don't ask for referrals from your prospects, customers and colleagues, then you are missing the boat.

Referrals are always stronger than cold calling whether it is in person (like I recommend) or on the phone because of the trust you have developed. Referrals are a connection you have with a new prospect which allows you to start off with a foot in the door. Referrals give you the ability to "piggy-back" off of a previous relationship you have already developed. Warm referrals are always better than a cold call.

For Free and For Fun

When asking for referrals, try to be specific and not too general. If your request is too broad, then chances are you will not get a good referral because it is difficult for people to think in generalities. If you say "Do you know 'anyone' that could use…?," then it would be very difficult for someone to come up with a name because the options are too vast. But if you were to say, "Who would you recommend I speak with at the hospital in Raleigh?" A "hospital in Raleigh" is very specific. The person you ask may not know anyone at the hospital in Raleigh, but they may know someone at the hospital in Durham.

Not only is a warm referral better than a cold call, but referrals also save you time. No one can know all of the prospects out there. I have gotten referrals I would never have come across or even thought about until my prospect had mentioned it. If you are set up to do five sales calls a week and you ask for referrals on each one, you will get two to three prospects to give you referrals. Normally when a person gives referrals, it is two to three people. This totals four to six people you did not even know existed with their contact information at the end of a week.

You know your numbers. How long does it take you to get four to six real callable numbers?

_____

_____

If you could get a full week's worth of appointments for the following week without any cold calling... how much time would you save?

_____

_____

After the sales call, where you get as far as you can, you then ask for referrals. I normally say something to the extent of, **"Well John, you've seen what I have and how I can HELP. I run most of my business off of referrals. Who else would you recommend I talk to in your industry to share how I can HELP?** Then I shut up and listen! In some instances, not only did the prospect tell me the names of some key contacts, but he also gave me coaching on the buying habits of the prospects as well. In short, the prospect gave me the ability to call another prospect and have a warm lead in without all of the leg work.

For Free and For Fun

When I get the referrals, I thank the prospect for the information and tell him I really appreciate him HELPing me. I then take out an appropriate little gift out of my sales bag to say thank you. I am there already so I might as well reward him right then. This allows me to ask the next question. **"John, thank you for the referrals, would you do me a favor? Would you mind emailing them to let them know I will be giving them a quick call to see how I can HELP?"** Very rarely have I ever had anyone tell me no. Doing this, when you call to make the appointment, gives you instant credibility with the new prospect. Many times I have called a new prospect and they have told me they have even spoken with John and they have been expecting my call.

A prospect expecting my call is powerful! I did not even know the guy, and he was expecting my call just because I did an appointment the week before and I asked a simple question. Not only can you get referrals right after the presentation, but there are many sources to tap into.

Existing Clients:

Your most recent new customer is your next testimonial.

When you have taken care of your customer, then you have the right to ask for a referral. The more you HELP your customer, the better the referrals will be because they trust you more. You are operating with absolute integrity. Your existing clients are a real life example of who you HELP. Chances are your customer knows other decision makers in his industry he can introduce you to. A great book to read is "The Referral of a Lifetime" by Timothy Templeton.

Referral Partners:

Question #1: Who are your customers? Are they sales managers? Are they homeowners? Are they companies with 50 employees?

Question #2: Who also sells to your customer? Invite this person to coffee or lunch. This person is a great resource for you and you are a great resource for them. Because you sell to the same customer there is a great opportunity for you to appropriately share your customer base. Of course this relationship is based on trust as well.

For Free and For Fun

When you do find out who your referral partners are then I would recommend getting to know them. Make it a point to learn more about how they HELP and how you can refer them to your customers and hopefully they will do the same.

BNI – Business Networking International (www.bni.com) is a great resource for bringing likeminded business men and women together weekly for the sole purpose of HELPing each other build their businesses.

Business Organizations:

Who are your customers again? Now figure out where your customers are. What organizations are they apart of? Where do they hang out? If your customer is an apartment community, then a good organization to join would be an apartment association. Be where your customers are. *If you sell sunglasses then go where it is sunny; go to the beach.*

Volunteering:

Volunteering will eventually lead to referrals and business. Eventually you will run into someone that will need your service. Through volunteering you will be able to develop great relationships and have exposure to people you may not have ever had a chance to meet any other way.

For example, while setting up for a church function, I happen to be working right next to Frank, a top manager of a major pharmaceutical company. I did not know who Frank was, but we were sweating together unfolding and placing out chairs. We struck up a conversation and asked each other about work. When we talked a little further, Frank thought more about how I HELP my customers. He asked me to come by the next day at 2 in the afternoon. Here I was at 7am, tired, out of breath, and sweating through my shirt and I was able make an appointment with one of my largest potential prospects. If I had not volunteered to set up chairs; I never would have been able to meet Frank anywhere else.

Even though volunteering will eventually lead to referrals and business; you have to go in with the expectation that you won't receive anything. If you

For Free and For Fun

volunteer only for business purposes, others will realize your motives and it will hurt you more professionally than HELP.

Only volunteer for organizations that:

1. You will add value to – you need to work and make an impact while you are there.
2. You find rewarding personally – if you get no value out of being there, you won't put your heart into it.
3. You can commit to 100% -- be accountable and dependable. If you say you will HELP, then you need to HELP.

Online Social Networks:

Another valuable resource for referrals is social networks. Nowadays your prospects are not only going to your website to learn about you and your company. Your prospects are also looking for third party resources to gain insight into who you are. Before, if you just had a website you had an advantage over your competitor who didn't but now everyone has a website. So, what is the next advantage? The next advantages are social networks like LinkedIn, Twitter, Plaxo, Facebook, and My Space, etc.

LinkedIn is the most popular business oriented social network. There are many others but I will give a little ink to LinkedIn. LinkedIn is a business/professional oriented online social network. LinkedIn allows you to set up your profile and give enough personal information to be a real person but not allowing you to talk about your recent boating trip or latest tattoo. As of this writing, there are over 25 million profiles on LinkedIn. Most of this LinkedIn information is from a seminar I attended that was conducted by Martin Brossman at *www.coachingsupport.com.*

There are a few very specific reasons I have found valuable having a LinkedIn profile.

1. Google searches – companies are "Googleling" you. LinkedIn is so entrenched with links that your LinkedIn account will almost always show up on the first page search results of Google. If not the number #1 spot on the first page then at a minimum in the top three. My personal LinkedIn account shows up as #1 if you Google "Christopher Morrissette."

2. LinkedIn allows your prospects and customers to have a third party reference about you that is business oriented with a small amount of personal information.

For Free and For Fun

LinkedIn allows your prospects to do a "background" check on you before they enter the sales cycle.

3. LinkedIn allows you to connect with referral partners. LinkedIn is a great resource as well as other local online social networks to allow you to connect with others who sell to your customers.

4. How many times have you walked in to get an order and your contact was no longer with the company. Where did they go? The employer usually will just tell you your contact is no longer with the company because most of the time they cannot elaborate. LinkedIn allows you to connect with your customers. Your main contact at a company will eventually move to another company. Your purchasing contact today will most likely not be there 5 years from now. LinkedIn allows you to follow and reconnect with your contact, when they get reestablished with another company. You get to maintain the relationship and hopefully pick up a new customer!

Do's and Don'ts of Online Social Networks:

<u>Do's:</u>

1. Do fill out your profile completely. If you are going to have a profile with a particular social network then it must be complete. If your profile is not complete, you will look like a ghost or people will assume you do not care how you look in public.

2. Do check in frequently, at least twice a week. If you start a profile and don't maintain contact, people will think you fell off the face of the earth or that you aren't in business anymore.

3. Do add value. When you "check in" add value in all of your communications. Look to give without getting and you will increase your respect and reputation in your online community.

For Free and For Fun

Don'ts:

1. Don't put anything on your profile you wouldn't want your spouse, parents or children to see. Remember you are setting up these networks to gain exposure to the world, not to "expose yourself to the world." Your colleagues and customers do not want to see your latest wild party or your newest piercing.

   This is also true if you are looking for a job. It is commonplace now for hiring personnel to look at your social networking profiles before an interview. You would be surprised at what people put online for the world to see.

   Remember— if you are online; you are in public.

2. Don't SELL on your profiles. Only look to HELP and give value to people.   It is OK to put links to your website that offers your products and services, but don't solicit on your profile.   It doesn't matter how good your multi-million dollar business opportunity is or if you really have the cure to cancer. When people read a commercial it makes them want to throw up.

3. Don't spend hours online finding and chatting with people. It is fine to check in with a long lost friend but remember you are cutting in to your work time and energy. You will spend some time initially setting up your profiles and learning how to navigate around the sites but don't lose track of reality.

   After the initial set up, I would recommend spending no more than 20 minutes a day checking in on ALL your profiles. To help with this you could set up your web browser to automatically open all of your social networking sites. When you finish checking in with one site then close that web page and move onto the next until you have looked at all of your profiles. Don't go back to the site until tomorrow.

4. Don't connect to everybody. You are still guilty by association here as well. If your profile is clean and neat and all of your "friends" have crazy profiles then the assumption will be you are crazy also. I wish this weren't true. I know this is not fair, but unfortunately this is reality.

For Free and For Fun

- 13 -

Let's Play Hangman!

Do you remember the game Hangman as we were growing up? Hangman is where your friend writes down a mystery word with all blanks while you try to guess all the letters and eventually the word. Don't guess a wrong letter. Why? Because you eventually miss enough and place a noose around the stick man and hang him. Hence Hangman!

There are tons of new technologies to choose from out there. From smart phones to text messaging; from landing sites for customer leads to electronic billboards; from email to instant messaging. Technology is a lot like Hangman. We try to guess what will be effective and what will not. When we guess wrong it is like putting a noose around our time and our wallets, crushing the life out of both.

My only advice is the less you have, the simpler it is to use, the better. There are two main questions to ask yourself when you are considering purchasing new technology.

For Free and For Fun

1. Can my prospect or customer use this to contact me for an appointment or an order?
2. Does it save me time?

If you can answer a resounding YES to both of these questions then the technology you are considering is absolutely necessary. If you answer NO or MAYBE then the technology is not important; it is just entertainment.

I personally use a smart phone which has email and text capability. With the email settings, I don't have it "pushed" through to my phone. I found this very distracting because whenever I got an email I felt the intense urge to see what type of "Spam" I got. Can you say "Crackberry?" This was interrupting my focus during the day, on sales calls and even dinner. I had to look to see who sent me an email. This wasted a lot of time and distracted my focus from the people most important to me.

Now I have my email set up where I have to manually go "grab" and download my messages. This way I can check my email at 12pm, after I am done with my morning to see if anything urgent came. I also check my email around 5pm to follow up on anything immediate and clear up any messages before I get home for the evening.

This allows me to stay connected to my customers and spend time with my family when I get home.

Trust me, if it is extremely urgent then you will get a phone call. Use technology to be as effective as possible but not to the point that it controls your life.

For Free and For Fun

- 14 -

What's Your Sign?

In the accounting world there are only two signs which mean anything. They are "+, plus" or "-, minus." You are "+ profits" or "- profits." Or you might know them as colors; in the red or the black. You are either above your budget or below your budget. You are either exceeding your sales target or sucking wind.

How are you doing right now? What's your sign? How many prospect calls do you need to make to be profitable? There is an easy process to figure this out.

What is your Magic Number?

Like Stephen Covey suggests, in his book *The 7 Habits of Highly Effective People*, you should begin with the end in mind. Start with where you want to finish and work backwards. This works whether you are an individual sales person running a territory or a sales manager responsible for a district or a multi-national company promising share holders a 10% return. Where do you want to be? How much money do you need to make?

For Free and For Fun

1. How much money do you need to make? $100,000?
    $200,000? $400,000? If you don't know how much
    you want/need to make then you will have to settle for
    whatever you end up with. If you are making all the
    money you need to make then you will have very little
    incentive to change and do more. What is your income
    expectation this year?

    _____

    _____

2. How much profit/commission do you make off of each
    new customer? Yes, I know it depends; everything
    depends. I know you make more money off some
    things than others. What is your average? Use your
    average number. Some sales positions are worth
    $1,000 in income for a new customer and some are
    worth $100. What is your average customer worth to
    you?
    What is your average customer commission value?

    _____

    _____

3. How many new customers/sales do you need? If you want to make $200,000 and your average commission for a new customer is $1,000 then you would need 200 new customers for the year.
    What is the number of new customer sales you need?

    _____

    _____

4. What is your closing percentage? Is it 50%? 30%? 10%? Don't know? You will get better with time learning your industry and increasing your skills. What is your closing percentage?

    _____

    (If you don't know your percentage, use 10%. Even a blind dog with a note in his mouth can sell 10% of his appointments. And yes, I really do feel like this sometimes.)

5. How many appointments do you need to make based on your closing percentage? If your closing percentage is 10% and you need 200 new customer sales to make your income target, then you need to do 2000 appointments. What is the number of appointments you need?

    _____

6. How many prospect calls do you need to make to get the number of appointments? With my system explained earlier, depending on the industry, I usually have 40% to 60% of cold calls end up in appointments booked. At 2000 appointments needed and only booking 25% of cold calls you would have to do 8000 prospect/cold calls. What is *your* number?

_____

7. How many prospect calls do you need to make daily? 8000 cold calls / 250 working days = 32 cold calls a day. This is your magic number!
Now, what is your magic number?

_____

This is your magic number. This is your sign. This is the number of prospect calls you need to do *daily* to make your number/profit/commission for the year. If you would like to admit it or not; you will live and die by this magic number. If you do this every day you will be successful and make money. If you do not do these prospect calls every day then you will fail. There are no other options. Your choice.

Is Your Magic Number Realistic?

The answer is ALWAYS Yes!

Is your magic number realistic? 32 cold calls a day is probably not realistic for most people over the course of "1 year." But doing 15 cold calls a day over "2 years" can be realistic for most. Over 3 years it is 10 calls a day and is very doable. Over 4 years it is very easy at 8 cold calls a day. Over 5 years it is 6 calls a day. Over 10 years it is 3 calls a day.

Your magic number is *always* realistic if you are willing to put enough time in. You may not be able to accomplish your income goal in one year but there are not too many reasons you can't accomplish it in two years. There is virtually no reason why you can't accomplish your income goal in three years. How long are you willing to give till you make your "Magic Number" realistic?

For Free and For Fun

- 15 -

Three Hours of Focus

There were two young Indians with the tribal Chief taking hunting lessons with a bow and arrow. The young hunters were learning how to focus and aim at their target. There was a 15 foot pole surrounded by a pond. At the top of the 15 foot pole was a large fish. The goal was to shoot the arrow into the eye of the fish on the pole while looking at the reflection of the fish in the pond. No easy feat.

The tribal Chief asked the first hunter what he sees. The first hunter answered, "I see green trees on the side of the pond, I see white clouds in the blue sky, I see the wind blowing through the trees and I see the fish on the pole. The chief then asked the second hunter what he sees. The second hunter replied solely, "I see the eye of the fish." When you are so focused on the eye of the fish, when you are so focused on what you want to accomplish, your goal is all you see. Then, and only then, will you hit your target.

For Free and For Fun

Einstein once said that he was not smarter than anyone else; he just stayed on the problem longer. When you know your magic number, you need to stay focused on it until you are done. I would urge you to do this before lunch. The reason before lunch, if you wait untill after lunch there will be many opportunities to distract you. With these distractions you will never get around to doing the most important activities. Before lunch it is much easier to maintain focus. Almost everything thrown at you can be put off till after lunch.

You will be bombarded throughout the day with:

1. Customer complaints

2. Customer issues

3. Proposal Requests

4. Employee issues

5. Family Member Calling

6. College Buddy Calling

7. Your Girlfriend or Boyfriend Calling

8. Delivering Product

9. Sales Presentations

10. Prospecting / Cold Calling

11. Following up on New Customers

12. Put another fun time waster here

13. Coworker or friend calling to see where you are going to lunch

The fact is very few of these activities make you more money. The only thing which makes you more money is HELPing more people. Now let's think about this. Out of all these things I mentioned above, what are the *easiest* things to do?

List them in order of easiest to most difficult:

1.   2.

3.   4.

5.   6.

7.   8.

9.   10.

11.   12.

For Free and For Fun

Now let's do the list again. Let's think about these activities in respect to your goals. What are the ***most important*** things to do?

List them in order of most important to least important:

1.   2.

3.   4.

5.   6.

7.   8.

9.   10.

11.   12.

Are both the easy and important lists the exact same? Why are they not the same? What is the *easiest thing* to do? What is the ***most important***? My point is if you do not do the most important things first *before* lunch then you will probably not do them at all.

Everything else is easier and more comfortable than the most important thing; prospecting and cold calling. Yes, even dealing with an angry customer is easier and more comfortable than making a cold call. Or at a minimum you will rationalize, "Well, I have to go see them or we will lose the business." Yes, you do have to go take care of the issue, but wait till after lunch or even better take the upset customer out to lunch! I have never been able to be mad at somebody while eating with them.

Do the most important things first.

For Free and For Fun

- 16 -

Are You a Boy Scout?

How Prepared Are You?

OK... you got the appointment. You arrived at Mr. Smith's office five minutes ahead of time. You are dressed properly. Are you ready to talk? Yes, you *think* so? Oh no. Remember the 6 P's? Prior Planning and Preparation Prevents Poor Results. Yeah, I know there are only 5 P's... but you will remember it. You need to live by the Boy Scout motto, "always be prepared." You have one shot to talk about what the prospect would like to talk about. Do not "wing it." If you go into an appointment unprepared the prospect will know it and you will blow it. You will waste his time and yours. Don't tell the prospect you can HELP them and not be able to carry it through. Don't cry wolf... be prepared.

Being prepared to go into your sales call is important but planning your day before you leave the house is even more important. If you don't have a plan then I would recommend you stay home and not leave until you do have a working plan.

You say, "Well, if I don't go out I won't make any money." You are right! You can't stay home. But if you do leave the house without a plan then you won't make any money either. I have personally left without a daily plan of who I needed to see and what I wanted to accomplish for the day. All I did was drive around aimlessly wondering what to do next. I found myself driving from one part of town to make a prospect call, and then going across town to do the second prospect call, wasting gas and time. The worse thing was that I actually thought I was accomplishing something and being productive. I believed my own BS! It would have been smarter and more productive to have done a sales call and then cold called in the same area. If you leave without a plan then you are wasting your time. You should stay home and watch TV; you will have the same results.

Daily Planning Tips

Some things to consider while developing a daily plan:

1. Do what is simple and easy for you. By the way, doing "nothing" for planning is probably the easiest but again it is <u>not</u> very effective. So find something which works but is not too difficult to maintain.

2. Be consistent and <u>do it daily</u>. It doesn't matter what you do just as long as you do it every day. You have to be consistent.

3. Plan your next day's activities before you go to bed. For some reason when you plan the night before your mind will think about your activities while you sleep. When you wake up you will be clear on your plan for the day.

For Free and For Fun

4. What is success today? Whether it is to make 20 cold calls or close 3 accounts this should be at the top of your list, so you look at it all day. The daily objective should be broken down from your yearly goals and your magic number. It is that simple. Your magic number will let you know you had a successful day when you had one. Your magic number will give you a daily goal to strive for.

 Most salespeople I run into do not know what a great day is. They think they had a great day by closing one new customer but never realize they need two new customers to hit their yearly goal. These salespeople don't see the discrepancy until September or October when they wonder why they are so far away from their yearly goal or budget. At this point they are too far away from their goal for it to be feasible for them to accomplish. Then they wonder why their boss gave them a bad performance or they are not making money. "Well," they think to themselves, "better start sandbagging for next year."

5. Some questions to answer for your daily plan:

   a. Where am I in respect to my goals?
      i. How much do I need to create in sales?
      ii. How many new customers do I need to HELP?

   b. What do I need to follow up from yesterday? Who do I need to call back?

   c. What presentations or proposals do I have?
      i. Am I prepared for those presentations?
      ii. What do I need to be prepared?

   d. Who do I need to see? How do I approach them?
      i. Cold Call?
      ii. Telephone Call?
      iii. Send them an Email?

   e. How much in new customer sales should I expect today?

For Free and For Fun

- 17 -

How Many Licks Does It Take?

Yeah, we all remember the commercial where the little boy asks the turtle, "How many licks to get to the center of a tootsie roll Tootsie Pop?" The turtle says "I don't know; I never made it without biting. Ask Mr. Owl." The little boy finds Mr. Owl to ask the same question. Mr. Owl grabs the Tootsie Pop and says lick "1," lick "2," lick "3," and then does a huge CHOMP. "Three." Then the narrator finishes the commercial, "How many licks does it take to get to the center of a Tootsie Pop? The world may never know."

How many prospecting/cold calls does it take to hit your goals? How many sales presentations does it take for you to be successful? "The world may never know." You can never really predict where your will sales come from. But if you do enough work the sales will be there.

The only thing you can control is your activity. Start by setting up a daily point system based on your goals to see what you need to accomplish for the day. With growing Easy Giving, I spend most of my time

For Free and For Fun

HELPing out new customers. Because of this, my personal point system is heavily weighted around prospecting and setting up new accounts. I have a personal goal of getting 20 points a day. These are how my activities are weighted.

- Prospecting / Cold Calling = 1 point

- Following up with a Customer = 1 point

- Networking Event = 1 point per *real* business contact

- Making an Appointment = 2 points

- One on One with a Referral Partner = 2 points

- Sales Presentations = 3 points

- Getting an Order from a New Customer = 4 points

If an activity does not fall into these above categories; prospecting, following up with a customer, getting a referral, making an appointment, doing a sales presentation, or getting an order from a new customer, then do not put much time into it. This point system will help keep you focused on the most important aspects of your business. If you spend time doing something else then you will be distracted from hitting your sales objective. Try to hit every category daily with 10 points a day in cold calling. Remember cold calling forces you to continue to build your prospecting pipeline and do activities which will keep your business growing.

This point system works because it inherently tells you what activity you need to be doing at any given moment. If you do not have any appointments for presentations or new customer sales then you need to make phone calls to make appointments. If you can't make any phone calls for appointments then you need to get referrals or start cold calling to fill up your prospect pipeline. It is very simple. The point system lets you know where you need to spend your time.

How many points do you need? What are you trying to accomplish? You can weight each activity in your work day to what is most valuable to your business. You may already have a huge book of business and you just want to maintain your business a little bit, then you can weight your points to following up with existing customers to be more valuable.

If you are trying to increase your offerings to existing customers, you could create other categories: number of customers seen, how many solutions were offered, or how much time did you spend with the customer, etc. You determine the points by determining what is most important to your business; this is where you need to spend your time. When you know where you need to spend your time then you can track your progress.

Working Exercise:

1. What are you trying to accomplish? There are only three things you can do with a customer. You can either:
   a. Retain them
   b. Increase your offerings to them
   c. Get a new customer

Which one is most important to your business right now?

_____

_____

_____

_____

_____

2. What are the top 4 or 5 most important activities to HELP you achieve what you are trying to accomplish?

_____

Points

_____

Points

_____

Points

_____

Points

_____

Points

3. Which activities are the most important? Give the most important activity 4 points and work your way back to the least important activity. Keep in mind the activities you have listed are all important or you would not have placed them on the list.

For Free and For Fun

4. This is not an excuse for you to not get the work done which needs to be done. For instance, if you have a customer complaint you should take care of it as soon as you can after lunch. Just because you don't have a category for customer complaints does not mean you should not take care of the customer.

5. You will have to tweak this over a period of time to truly figure out if you are spending your time in the most valuable and important areas. This point system will give a good outline and game plan to begin working with.

- 18 -

Let the Games Begin!

Once you have decided what is important to you, you now have an easy way to track your daily progress that is related to your yearly goal. The next step is you will need to find a way to encourage yourself to continue doing the most important items for 21 days till they become a habit. It seems the most important items on your "to do" list also would be the most uncomfortable or the least amount of fun. So you will have to find a way to make it fun.

In the spirit of having fun you are going to have to make this a game within yourself. If you are begrudging doing the things which are the most important, you are not going to be successful because you will not do them. If you make it fun, the more you will do, the more you keep up your enthusiasm and the more you increase your chances of success. I would recommend starting out small. If you ever watch football not only do they celebrate winning the game but they also celebrate every score along the way. Where do you think the "Touch

Down Dance" came from? Or baseball, when a player hits a home run all the teammates meet the batter at the plate to celebrate. You have to celebrate your small successes. With celebration is encouragement and the energy to help you do more. Be creative.

If you have determined prospecting is the most important activity, you might have to do a lot of cold calls to get comfortable. So do five cold calls before lunch and reward yourself with a nice thick cheeseburger at your favorite restaurant. Or if you are motivated negatively, don't let yourself eat lunch until you do five cold calls. Start out with five cold calls to work your endurance and confidence up. After you and a friend do ten cold calls the first time, go out and celebrate. Go go-karting, go to the arcade or batting cage, etc. just enjoy your small success.

The goal is to work yourself up to your magic number. And after a year, at the very longest two, you will not have to do another cold call ever again. How much is a customer worth to you? You will get better over time and your appointment and close ratio will increase dramatically by doing enough work to learn what you are really doing which is HELPing. If you do enough work and HELP enough people get what they want you cannot HELP but be successful!

Sales managers, my business HELPs companies get a greater return on their sales promotions and incentives. If you would like HELP and ideas, feel free to contact me at chris@givingisez.com or go to www.givingisez.com. There are many ways to create a simple tiered system for performance with employee work habits which will make your team successful.

For Free and For Fun

- 19 -

The Sales Slump – Nobody Loves Me

Are you in a slump? The only way to get out of a slump is to *work* out of it. If you are in a slump it can be mentally and emotionally draining. You are thinking too much. Chances are you playing back in your mind all of the people who say they do not want or need you. Nobody loves you.

You have to do a "check up from the neck up." You need to replay of all of your past successes. You have to continually remind yourself your work habits are going to be fruitful.

1. Replay in your mind all of your previous sales successes:

    - the moment you introduced yourself on a cold call
    - how receptive the prospect was when you called back to ask for the appointment to HELP them
    - the back and forth dialogue of the presentation
    - the prospect's face lighting up when they finally realized they did need you

- and play back in your mind when you asked for the order and the customer signed the contract

2. Leaders Are Readers –

   a. Read biographies of great men. All successful men and women have a story that has highs and lows. No one is successful all the way through life. Biographies are always a struggle to victory story. Not only are biographies inspirational but they are educational as well. You are learning from men and women that are successful.

   b. Read as much as you can about sales, personality types, and leadership. In the end, the more you can relate to people and communicate your ideas effectively, the more money you will make and the happier you will be.

      Remember, Charlie "Tremendous" Jones – *"The only difference between who you are today and the person you will be in five years will come from the books you read and the people you associate with"*

   Go to www.forfreeandforfun.com for a recommended reading list. I have also put a recommended reading list in the appendix of this book for quick access.

3. Read daily motivational quotes. Quotes of successful people help you think.

4. See yourself being successful. Image what life is going to be like at Christmas for your children. Imagine the vacation in Hawaii you will take with your family or the feeling of being out of debt. See yourself living in your dream home.

"Continually remind yourself of your past successes and believe in your vision of who you will become in the future and this will give you all of the energy you will need to continue."

Christopher Morrissette

For Free and For Fun

Summary

The most important part of work is the *work*. When you look for results for results sake, you will fail. You have to work "For Free and For Fun," if you are going to be successful in anything. When you go out, and HELP others and plant seed in the ground, after a few years you will look back on the harvest you created and marvel at where all of these customers came from and wonder where they were in the beginning. Your customers were always there; you just had to prove yourself capable of caring for them. You had to prove yourself worthy.

By making daily connections either through cold calling or referrals you will grow your business to heights never imagined if you just continue and do not quit. Just continue planting and continue HELPing and you will reap a harvest pressed down shaken and spilling over.

For Free and For Fun

There is a famous quote by Mark Twain:

"Dance like nobody's watching; love like you have never been hurt. Sing like nobody's listening; live like it's heaven on earth."

I would like to add one line:

"HELP like you already have everything to give away."

Remember...

For Free and For Fun!

Appendixes

<u>Cold Calling Process</u>

I. **Attitude**
   a. I am human; I am talking to another human therefore BE HUMAN.
   b. Relax – it is only a cold call the first time, then they know you.
   c. I am here to HELP increase the prospects quality of life.

II. **Thought Process**
   a. They need me to HELP, I can HELP them with:
      i. Time
      ii. Money
      iii. Stress
      iv. People
      v. Lead time
      vi. Quality
   b. Why am I calling them if I don't think I can HELP?

III. Purpose

a. Meet the gate keeper to find out whom to make an appointment with.

b. Talk to the decision maker to make an appointment.

IV. What's Your Sign; What's Your "Magic Number"

a. How much do you need to make?

b. How much is a customer worth?

c. How many customers do you need?

d. How many prospect/ cold calls do you need to make daily?

e. Are you willing to do your magic number? Is it worth it to you?

V. The Game

a. Keep Score – how many points do you need?

b. Are you working or getting distracted?

c. Reward yourself – celebrate the small successes.

d. Cheer when other people score as well.

e. In a slump – think back on all of the successful sales you have had and remember every moment from the beginning of the introduction to the sale.

Recommended Reading

Some great Biographies:

- Abraham Lincoln
- Benjamin Franklin
- Ryan Allis – *Zero to One Million*
- Warren Buffet
- Donald Trump
- Farrah Gray – *Reallionaire*

Some great Sales Books:

- Anything by Jeffrey Gitomer – www.buygitomer.com
- Brian Tracy -- *The Psychology of Selling*
- Tom Hopkins – *How to Master the Art of Selling*
- Timothy Templeton – *Referral of a Lifetime*

Some great Leadership/Management Books:

- John Maxwell – *The 21 Irrefutable Laws of Leadership*
- Stephen Covey – *7 Habits of Highly Effective People*
- Jim Collins – *Good to Great*